HEAVEN

PURGATORY

HELL

HEAVEN

PURGATORY

HELL

Paul Edmond Beaulieu

Copyright 2013 © Paul Edmond Beaulieu

All rights reserved.

No part of this book may be reproduced in any form or by any electronic or mechanical means, including all information storage and retrieval systems, without written permission from the author.

Reviewers may quote brief passages in review.

Library and Archives Canada Cataloguing in Publication

Beaulieu, Paul Edmond, 1947-, author
   Heaven, purgatory, hell / Paul Edmond Beaulieu.

Co-published by: Lulu.com.
ISBN 978-0-9809572-6-6 (pbk.)

   1. Future life--Christianity. I. Title.

BT903.B42 2013   236'.2   C2013-902511-1

Design and layout by: Ignatius Fay, PhD

Published by: Ignatius Fay, PhD and Lulu.com

Copies of this work may be purchased online at:
http://www.lulu.com

Dedicated to:

Our Lady, Mary, Mother Of God

Luke 1:28
Upon arriving, the angel said to her, "Rejoice, O highly favored daughter! The Lord is with you. Blessed are you among women."

Acknowledgments

Three Catholic priests from Sudbury, Ontario were kind enough to proofread the draft of this manuscript to ensure that the material herein does not contravene the teachings of the Catholic Church. I am grateful and indebted to them for their assistance.

I deeply appreciate the efforts of my friend, Ignatius Fay, for his technical assistance, editing and page layout.

Contents

Acknowledgments	vii
Preface	1
Eternity	5

Chapter 1 Heaven — 9
Who will go to Heaven?	11
How do the chosen get to Heaven?	17
What is it like in Heaven?	19

Chapter 2 Purgatory — 25
A Reflection on Purgatory	27
Who will go to Purgatory?	29
What is it like in Purgatory?	31

Chapter 3 Hell — 33
A Reflection on Hell	35
Who will go to hell?	36
How do the condemned get to hell?	45
What is it like in hell?	48

Chapter 4 Recommendations on — 53
Recommendations	55

Chapter 5 Spiritual Thoughts — 61
Love	63
What we choose to believe	64
Forgiveness	71
Scapular	74
Steps to Serenity and Peace	75
Teaching on Contraception	77
One Master	78
An Interesting Article	79

Conclusion — 81

Preface

The purpose of writing this book is to encourage my family, friends and acquaintances to reflect upon how a way of life effects eternity. Why was I inspired to do this? I believe that the occasional contemplation of eternity is an effective method for developing spiritual life. This heightened awareness leads to increased inner strength, true hope and genuine contentment. I hope this work will encourage readers to set aside some time to reflect on eternity.

My perception of our present time is that we have become an extremely busy people. A continual and growing demand is placed on our time to be successful and to provide a normal lifestyle for ourselves and our families, all the while squeezing in other activities. Especially now, with cuts in personnel and in wages being widespread, both husbands and wives are increasingly required to work. The pace of technology demands that we continually upgrade our skills, usually on our own time, or we find ourselves left behind or unemployed. When a bit of time becomes available, we have been trained to turn to the television as a means of entertainment and relaxation. These situations make it very difficult to set time aside for reflection on our human and spiritual lives, the lack of which has a direct effect on our eternal destiny.

I believe this situation, without our awareness, prevents us from meditating on the mysteries of life, like eternity. We hear an increasing number of Christians say there is no Purgatory or Hell, although our Lord has clearly instructed us to the contrary in his Word and by his Church. Our tendency is to push these thoughts aside because to admit the reality of Purgatory and Hell is too challenging or that they do not conform to what our modern world would label as 'Scientific' or 'Modern.'

As taught by scripture and supported by our Church, our deaths will reveal our eternal destiny. The way of life we choose will be the determining factor of our final judgement. The outcome will be one of three possibilities: *Eternal Blessed Heaven,* where there is no sadness, no tears, only eternal happiness; *Purgatory,* a temporary place of physical and psychological suffering to eradicate the remnants of our venial sins, to finish atoning for the sins we have committed and that have been forgiven, but for which we have not made restitution while on earth; *Eternal Hell,* permanent torture and suffering beyond our comprehension, where there is never any hope, for those who have turned against God and chosen to live contrary to his call during their earthly life.

I have attempted to describe what eternity will be like for humans by dealing with *Heaven,*

Purgatory and *Hell.* Three questions are being posed for each:
1) Who will go there?
2) How do we get there?
3) What is it like there?

I have chosen scripture as a source for the answers. This book includes every line in the new testament that I perceive pertains to answering the three chosen questions.

Final thought! God has willed so very much that we understand that our post-death judgement will result in our going to Heaven, Purgatory or Hell. Not only are they mentioned often in scripture, but the message of their existence has been communicated to us throughout the centuries by our Church, the apparitions of numerous Saints and Our Lady's frequent visits at various places on earth.

Eternity

Think
Mortal Man, your body will soon turn into dust,
but you have an immortal soul but you never
think about it!

Study, meditate deeply on this grand word:
Eternity!

Oh man, what will you say one day?
What will it hold for you, this inevitable
Eternity!

Oh! how long! how profound! how immense and
infinite in its goodness and its iniquity, this queen
of all centuries, this neverending and always living
Eternity!

For the true Christian, it is infinite in its
goodness.
For the sinner, it is infinite in its iniquity, this
neverending
Eternity!

Count as many millions of years as there are leaves
in the trees in the forests,
as grains of sand on all the beaches,

as blades of grass on the plains,
as drops of water in the ocean,
as stars in the firmament.
Count again — Count forever:
Your numbers are nothing when compared to
the incomprehensible eternity!
Eternity! Eternity!

A day is coming when the sun will have been extinguished, the world will have been consumed, the human race will have come to an end, the living and the dead will have been judged, centuries upon centuries will have passed, an abyss of time will have passed since the existence of life, and passed so fast; this life will be infinitely remote, like stars that are only perceptable to the eye through great concentration, like a thought that has almost vanished…And this will continue, and it will never end
Eternity for Eternity!

For it will last forever, it never ends!
Oh always! Oh never! Oh eternity!
If heaven is **ETERNITY**,
what incomprehensible happiness!
Always truth and virtue, life and joy,
happy people and angels.

Always God
To meditate, to love, to possess, to bless, always.
And no tears, no death, no sorrow, no anger, no pain! **EVER!** (Apoc, xxiv, 4)
But if I spend **ETERNITY** in Hell,

appalling misfortune!
Always the remorse that eats away;
Always the fire that burns;
Always the tears that fall;
Always the teeth that grind;
Always the demons that torture;
Always the curse of God;
Never a ray of daylight that brings joy!
Never a moment of rest!
Never a drop of water that refreshes!
Never a glimpse of hope! Never! Never!

Oh Always! Oh never! Oh Eternity!

Mortal, who has an immortal soul, eternity exists.
Do you think about it?…No.
And that eternity is for you.

It doesn't matter if you believe in it! If it does not exist, what risk to you living well?…
But if it does exist, what consequences your foolish error will have!
For, it does exist, and you are on the edge of this eternity; and in a few days, there will be nothing left:
Of all the PLEASURES that you enjoy;
Of all the AFFAIRS that occupy you;
Of all this LIFE that abuses you;
there will be only
Eternity!
Eternity and your **labors** and their **fruits**;
Alas, the pleasures of the sinner will have passed;
but his pain will remain.

And the pain of the just will have passed;
but his goodness will remain.
Therefore, either the
pleasures during your life
with their eternal pain,
or the pain during your life
with the joys of eternity.

Choose…
Oh Eternity! Oh Eternity!

I have chosen. I want it to be heaven.
I want to pass you to God.
God eternal, Oh my sovereign judge! Seized with fear,
I throw myself to your feet; in face of your eternity, my only recourse is in your grandiose goodness and in the armature of my contrition.
Forgive me, forgive me for exposing myself to sin, running the risk of losing you for eternity. I believe in you and in eternity, I hope in you, and from you I seek happiness for eternity. I love you and want to love you for all eternity.
Hit me, cut me, burn me, do not spare me any suffering during my life, but save me, save me for eternity.
Without delay, I wish to make a sincere confession of all my sins, and apply myself to living a pious and holy life, to love and bless you in joyous eternity! Amen.

*(Translated from the French original
by J.-Omer Plante, 1929)*

Chapter 1

Heaven

Who will go to Heaven?

Matthew 7:21 the one who does the will of the father.

Matthew 10:41 He who welcome a prophet because he bears a name of a prophet receives a prophet's reward; he who welcomes a holy man because he is known to be holy receives a holy man's reward.

Matthew 10:42 And I promise you that whoever gives a cup of cold water to one of these lowly ones because he is a disciple will not want for his reward.

Matthew 16:27 When he does, he will repay each man according to his conduct.

Matthew 18:01 Who is of greatest importance in the kingdom of God? He called a little child over and stood him in their midst and said "I assure you, unless you change and become like little children, you will not enter the Kingdom of God. Whoever makes himself lowly, becoming like this child, is of greatest importance in that heavenly reign."

Matthew 19:28 Moreover, every one who has given up home, brother or sister, father or mother, wife or children or property for my sake will receive many times as much and inherit everlasting life.

Matthew 20:22 You do not know what you are asking. Can you drink the cup I am to drink of? We can they said.

Matthew 21:31 I assure you that tax collectors and prostitutes are entering the kingdom of God before you.

Matthew 21:43 For this reason, I tell you, the kingdom of God will be taken away from you and given to a nation that will yield a rich harvest.

Matthew 22:10 The servant went out into the byroads and rounded up every-one they met, bad as well as good.

Matthew 24:13 The man who holds out to the end, however, is the one who will see salvation.

Matthew 24:46 Happy that servant whom his master discovers at work on his return!

Matthew 25:10 While they went off to buy it the groom arrived, and the ones who were ready went in to the wedding with him.

Matthew 25:21 Since you were dependable in a small matter I will put you in charge of larger affairs. Come share your master's joy!

Matthew 25:46 and the just to eternal life.

Marc 10:21 Go and sell what you have and give to the poor; you will then have treasure in heaven.

Marc 10:25 It is easier for a camel to pass through a needle's eye than for a rich man to enter the kingdom of God.

Marc 10:29–30 I give you my word, there is no one who has given up home, brother or sister, mother or father, children or property, for me and for the gospel who will not receive in this present age a hundred times as many homes, brother and sisters, mothers, children and property - and persecution besides - and in the age to come, everlasting life.

Marc 12:33–34 Yes, to love him with all your heart, with all our thoughts and with all our strength, and to love our neighbor as ourselves is worth more than any burnt offering or sacrifice. Jesus approved the insight of this answer and told him, "You are not far from the reign of God".

Marc 13:13 Nonetheless, the man who holds out to the end is the one who will come through safe.

Marc 16:16 The man who believes in it and accepts baptism will be saved.

Marc 16:20 Later on it was through them that Jesus himself sent out from east to west the sacred and immortal proclamation of eternal salvation.

Luke 6:20–23 Blest are you poor; the reign of God is yours.
Blest are you who hunger; you shall be filled.
Blest are you who are weeping; you shall laugh.
Blest shall you be when men hate you, when they ostracize you and insult you and proscribe your name as evil because of the Son of Man. On the day they do so, rejoice and exult, for your reward shall be great in heaven.

Luke 9:24 and whoever loses his life for my sake will save it.

Luke 9:48 Whoever welcomes this little child on my account welcomes me, and whoever welcomes me welcomes him who sent me; for the least one among you is the greatest.

Luke 12:8 I tell you, whoever acknowledges me before men - the Son of Man will acknowledge him before the angels of God.

Luke 12:15 A man may be wealthy, but his possessions do not guarantee him life.

Luke 12:40 Be on your guard therefore. The Son of Man will come when you lest expect him.

Luke 12:43 That servant is fortunate whom his master finds busy when he returns.

Luke 13:29 People will come from the east and from the west, from the north and south, and will take their place at the feast in the Kingdom of God.

Luke 14:13–14 No, when you have a reception, invite beggars and the cripple, the lame and the blind. You should be pleased that they cannot repay you, for you will be repaid in the resurrection of the just.

Luke 16:13 You cannot give yourself to God and money.

Luke 17:29 I solemnly assure you, there is no one who has left home or wife or brothers, parents or children, for the sake of the kingdom of God who will not receive a plentiful return in this age and life everlasting in the age to come.

Luke 23:42–43 Jesus, remember me when you enter upon your reign. And Jesus replied I assure you, this day you will be with me in paradise.

John 3:18 Whoever believes in him avoids condemnation

John 5:24 I solemnly assure you, the man who hears my word and has faith in him who sent me possesses eternal life.

John 6:40 Indeed, this is the will of my Father, that everyone who looks upon the son and believes in him shall have eternal life.

John 6:54 He who feeds on my flesh and drinks my blood has life eternal

John 13:36 I am going where you cannot follow me now; later on you shall come after me

John 14:4 You know the way that leads where I go.

John 14:5 No one comes to the Father but through me

2 Corinthians 9:6 he who sows bountifully will reap bountifully.

Galatians 6:7 A man will reap only what he sows.

Philippians 3:20 As you well know, we have our citizenship in heaven; it is from here that we await the coming of our savior, the Lord Jesus Christ.

2 Timothy 2:11–12 If we have died with him we shall also live with him; if we hold out to the end we shall also reign with him.

Hebrew 4:6 Therefore since it remains for some to enter,

Hebrew 5:9 He became the source of eternal salvation for all who obey him,

Hebrew 11:16 Wherefore God is not ashamed to be called their God, for he has prepared a city for them.

Revelation 19:9 Happy are they who have been invited to the wedding feast of the lamb

Revelation 21:7 He who wins the victory shall inherit these gifts; I will be his God and he shall be my son.

Revelation 21:27 Only those shall enter whose names are inscribed in the book of the living kept by the lamb.

Revelation 22:12 I bring with me the reward that will be given to each man as his conduct deserves.

How do the chosen get to Heaven?

Matthew 13:30 then gather the wheat into my barn.

Matthew 13:49 That is how it will be at the end of

the world. Angels will go out and separate the wicked from the just

Matthew 16:27 The Son of Man will come with his Father's glory accompanied by his angels.

Matthew 25:34 The King will say to those on his right "Come, you have my Father's blessing! Inherit the kingdom prepared for you from the creation of the world."

Matthew 27:53 Many bodies of Saints who had fallen asleep were raised

Marc 13:27 He will dispatch his angels and assemble his chosen from the four winds, from the farthest bounds of earth and sky.

Luke 13:29 People will come from the East and from the West, from the North and from the South, and will take their place at the feast in the kingdom of God.

Luke 13:30 Some who are last will be first and some who are first will be last.

Luke 24:51 As he blessed, he left them, and was taken up to heaven.

John 5:28-29 for the hour is coming in which all those in their tombs shall hear his voice and come forth. Those who have done right shall rise to live.

John 6:40 Him I will raise on the last day

John 6:54 and I will raise him up on the last day.

Romans 2:5–7 God will be revealed, when he will repay every man for what he has done: eternal life to those who strive for glory, honor, and immortality by patiently doing right;

2 Corinthians 5:10 The lives of all of us are to be revealed before the tribunal of Christ so that each one may receive his recompense, good or bad, according to his life in the body.

2 Timothy 4:8 From now on a merited crown awaits me; on that day the Lord, just judge that he is, will award it to me - but not only to me, but to all who have looked for his appearing with eager longing.

What is it like in Heaven?

Mathew 5:19 That is why whoever breaks the least significant of these commands and teaches others to do so shall be called least in the kingdom of God.

Matthew 13:12 To the man who has, more will be given until he grows rich;

Matthew 13:43 Then the saints will shine like the sun in their Father's kingdom.

Matthew 18:01 "Whoever makes himself lowly, becoming like this child, is of greatest importance in that heavenly reign."

Matthew 19:28 I give you my solemn word, in the new age when the Son of Man takes his seat upon a throne befitting his glory, you who have followed me shall likewise take your place on twelve thrones to judge the twelve tribes of Israel.

Matthew 19:29 and the last shall come first.

Matthew 20:21–23 Promise me that these sons of mine will sit, one at your right side and the other at your left, in your kingdom. He told them " From the cup I drink of, you shall drink. But sitting at my right hand or my left is not mine to give. That is for those whom it has been reserved by my Father."

Matthew 22:30 When people rise from the dead, they neither marry nor are given in marriage but live like angels in heaven.

Matthew 25:21 Since you were dependable in a small matter I will put you in charge of larger affairs. Come share your master's joy!

Marc 12:25 When people rise from the dead, they neither marry nor are given in marriage but live like angels in heaven.

Marc 16:20 and inherent the spiritual and immortal glory and justification in heaven.

Luke 6:38 For the measure you measure with will be measured back to you.

Luke 13:18–19 What does the reign of God resemble? To what shall we liken it? It is like a mustard seed which a man took and planted in his garden. It grew and became a large shrub and the birds of the air nested on it's branches.

Luke 15:7 I tell you, there will likewise be more joy in heaven over one repentant sinner than over ninety-nine righteous people who have no need to repent.

John 14:2 In my Father's house there are many dwelling places;

1 Corinthians 2:9 "Eye has not seen, ear has not heard, nor has it so much as dawned on man what God has prepared for those who love him."

Romans 2:10 But there will be honor, and peace for everyone who has done good,

Philippians 3:21 He will give a new form to this lowly body of ours and remake it according to the pattern of his glorified body, by his power to subject everything to himself.

Revelation 3:7 who opens and no one can close,

Revelation 7:16 Never again shall they know hunger or thirst, nor shall the sun or heat beat down on them,

Revelation 7:17 and God will wipe every tear from their eyes.

Revelation 15:2–3 I then saw something like a sea of glass mingle with fire. On the sea of glass were standing those who had won the victory over the beast and its image, and also the number that signified its name. They were holding the harps used in worshiping GOD, and they sang the song of Moses, the servant of GOD, and the song of the Lamb.

Revelation 21:1 Then I saw a new heaven and a new earth.

Revelation 21:3 This is God's dwelling among men. He shall dwell with them and they shall be his people and he shall be their God who is always with them.

Revelation 21:4 He shall wipe every tear from

their eyes, and there shall be no more death or morning, crying out or pain, for the former world has passed away.

Revelation 22:4–5 They shall see him face to face and bear his name on their forehead. The night shall be no more. They will need no light from lamps or the sun, for the Lord God shall give them light, and they shall reign forever.

Chapter 2

Purgatory

Purgatory

A Reflection on Purgatory

During our modern time, many people doubt the existence of Purgatory. To show its reality, let us look at four sources by which our God communicates this truth to us.

The Bible
Numerous quotes make statements similar to: *2 Maccabees 12:46* "Thus he made atonement for the dead that they might be freed from this sin."

The Mass
Every day for centuries, the faithful have prayed for the souls of our departed brothers and sisters at every Mass said on our planet. The following is the prayer said by the priest and the faithful during Mass. "Remember, Lord, those who have died and have gone before us marked with the sign of faith, especially those for whom we now pray…May these and all who sleep in Christ find in your presence light, happiness and peace." The persistence of this prayer lends weighty support to the belief of the existence of Purgatory. If the departed are not in Purgatory, then they do not need prayers, they cannot benefit from our prayers.

The Church Teachings and Holy Tradition

The Church teaches as a revealed truth that the souls of the just who, while in this life, have failed to pay in full their debt to God's justice are cleansed in Purgatory to prepare them for admission to Heaven. Since the Church speaks infallibly in the name of God, we know therefore that God himself testifies, through the Church, to the existence of Purgatory.

The Catholic Church has defined the existence of Purgatory in the Decree of Union drawn up at the Council of Florence in 1439, and again at the Council of Trent (1545–1563). Through these deliberations, the existence of Purgatory was verified by the statement: "The Catholic Church, instructed by the Holy Ghost, has from Sacred Scripture and the ancient tradition of the Fathers, taught in Sacred Councils, and very recently in this Ecumenical Synod, that there is a Purgatory, and that the souls therein detained are helped by the suffrages of the faithful, but principally by the acceptable sacrifice of the altar."

The Communion of Saints

Apparitions of souls in Purgatory to persons still living (allowed by our Lord) have been numerous during the Christian era. No one can deny the possibility or, in fact, the reality of such apparitions. They are frequent occurrences in the lives of the Saints. The testimonies of theologians and historical documents are no less numerous or convincing. Many of these apparitions have been witnessed by saints, people of great integrity and intelligence with sound judgement, keen intellect and demonstrated common sense.

A common theme in every single one of these visits is their descriptions of intense, severe physical and mental suffering endured by these souls. They inform us we can relieve their suffering and shorten their time allotted in Purgatory by our prayers and, especially, by our offering of the Mass. We also become aware of the rigors of divine justice.

Note
Recommended book—*Purgatory Explained By the Lives and Legends of the Saints* by FR. F. X. Schouppe, S.J.

Who will go to Purgatory?

Matthew 11:24 I assure you, it will go easier for Sodom than for you on the day of judgment.

Matthew 12:32 Whoever says anything against the Son of Man will be forgiven, but whoever says anything against the Holy Spirit will not be forgiven, either in this age or in the age to come.

Mathew 12:36 I assure you, on judgement day every man will be held accountable for every unguarded word they speak.

Matthew 16:27 The Son of Man will come with his Father's glory accompanied by his angels. When he does, he will repay each man according to his conduct.

Mark 12:40 it is they who will receive the severest sentence.

Luke 13:30 Some who are last will be first and some who are first will be last.

2 Corinthians 9:6 He who sows sparingly will reap sparingly,

Galatians 4:30 Cast out slave girl and son together; for the slave girl's son shall never be an heir on equal terms with the son of one born free.

Galatians 6:7 A man will reap only what he sows.

Hebrew 2:2 and all transgression and disobedience receive its due punishment,

Hebrew 12:25 how much greater punishment will be ours if we turn away from him who speaks from heaven!

Revelation 2:23 I will give each of you what your conduct deserves.

What is it like in Purgatory?

Matthew 5:26 I warn you, you will not be released until you have paid the last penny.

Matthew 18:34 Then in anger the master handed him over to the torturers until he paid back all that he owed.

Luke 6:38 For the measure you measure with will be measured back to you.

Luke 12:47–48 The slave who knew his master's wishes but did not prepare to fulfill them will get a severe beating, whereas the one who did not know them and who nonetheless deserved to be flogged will get off with fewer stripes.

Luke 12:59 I warn you, you will not be released from there until you have paid the last penny.

1 Corinthians 3:11–15 No one can lay a foundation other than the one that has been laid, namely Jesus Christ. If different ones build on this foundation with gold, silver, precious stones, wood, hay or straw, the work of each will be made clear. The Day will disclose it. That day will make its appearance with fire, and fire will test the quality of each man's works. If the building a man has raised on this foundation still stands, he will receive his recompense; if a man's building burns, he will suffer loss. He himself will be saved, but only as one fleeing through fire.

Chapter 3

Hell

A Reflection on Hell

For the past while, we have heard many people from varied backgrounds and places describing their 'Near Death Experiences.' These persons have actually died and been pronounced dead by a doctor; the heart and respiratory system have actually stopped for an extended period of time, up to thirty minutes. Miraculously they have come back to life. Their minute-by-minute accurate descriptions of what went on around them leave no doubt in anybody's mind that, while dead, these persons had an awareness and comprehension of what was happening in their surroundings.

All these persons relate one of two experiences. The first is seeing and going through a tunnel, sometimes seeing loved ones that have passed away before them, sometimes being greeted by Jesus. They variously experience God's love, the realization of going to a place of eternal happiness, peace and well-being.

The second is encountering the smell of smoke and fire, seeing persons in torturous conditions, and being aware that those persons will never leave that place. Recently, I heard the testimony of a man on TV who had this experience. He was a gangster, a bad person. One day, during a fight, he was stabbed. Attending paramedics pronounced him dead, later confirmed by the doctor. The gangster said that, while in the ambulance, he smelled smoke. He thought that the ambulance was on fire. Then he saw hell and persons whom he had known and who had died before him. They were burning and in a torturous state. Then he heard a person in hell say to him: 'Do not come here. Once here, there is no way out, ever.' Moments later, he came back to life. This man became a preacher, a very caring person and is sharing his experience.

Who will go to hell?

Matthew 7:21 None of those who cry out,'Lord Lord,' will enter into the Kingdom of God but only the one who does the will of the Father.

Matthew 10:28 Rather, fear him who can destroy the body and the soul in Gehenna.

Mathew 12:32 but whoever says anything against the Holy Spirit will not be forgiven, either in this age or in the age to come

Matthew 15:13 Every planting not put up by my heavenly Father will be uprooted

Matthew 15:13 If one blind man leads another, both will be in the pit.

Matthew 16:26 What profit would a man show if he were to gain the whole world and destroy himself in the process?

Matthew 19:30 Many who are first shall come last.

Matthew 23:33 How can you escape condemnation in Gehenna.

Matthew 24:47-51 I assure you, he will be put in charge of all his property. But if the servant is worthless and tells himself,"My master is a long time in coming and begins to beat his fellow servants, to eat and drink with drunkards, that man's master will return when he is not ready and least expects him. He will punish him severely and settle with him as is done with hypocrites. There will be wailing and grinding of teeth.

Matthew 26:24 woe to the man by whom the Son of Man is betrayed. Better for him if he had never been born.

Marc 3:29 but whoever blasphemes against the Holy Spirit will never be forgiven. He carries the guilt of his sin without end.

Marc 8:38 If anyone in this faithless and corrupt age is ashamed of me and my doctrine, the Son of Man will be ashamed of him when he comes with the holy angels in his Father's glory.

Marc 9:42 But it would be better if anyone who leads astray one of these simple believers were to be plunged in the sea with a great milestone fastened around his neck.

Marc 9:43 If your hand is your difficulty, cut it off! Better for you to enter life maimed than to keep both hands and enter Gehenna with its unquenchable fire.

Marc 9:45 If your foot is your undoing, cut it off! Better for you to enter life crippled than to be thrown into Gehenna with both feet!

Marc 9:47 If your eye is your downfall, tear it out! Better for you to enter the kingdom of God with one eye than to be thrown with both eyes into Gehenna,

Marc 10:15 I assure you that whoever does not accept the reign of God like a little child shall not take part in it.

Marc 16:16 the man who refuses to believe in it will be condemned.

Luke 3:7 You brood of vipers! Who told you to flee from the wrath to come.

Luke 6:24–26 But woe to you rich, for your consolation is now.
Woe to you who are full; you shall go hungry.

Woe to you who laugh now; you shall weep in your grief.
Woe to you when all speak well of you.

Luke 6:38 For the measure you measure with will be measured back to you.

Luke 9:24 Whoever would save his life will lose it.

Luke 9:25 What profit does he show who gains the whole world and destroys himself in the process?

Luke 9:26 If a man is ashamed of me and my doctrine, the Son of Man will be ashamed of him when he comes in his glory and that of his Father and his holy angels.

Luke 9:62 Whoever puts his hand to the plow but keeps looking back is unfit for the reign of God.

Luke 11:23 He who is not with me is against me.

Luke 12:04–05 Do not be afraid of those who kill the body and can do no more. Fear him who has power to cast into Gehenna after he has killed.

Luke 12:09 But the man who has disowned me in the presence of men will be disowned in the presence of the angels of God

Luke 12:10 whoever blasphemes the Holy Spirit will never be forgiven.

Luke 12:15 A man may be wealthy, but his possession do not guarantee him life.

Luke 12:45–46 But if the servant says to himself "My master is taking time about coming, and begins to abuse the housemen and the servant girls, to eat and drink and get drunk, that servant's master will come back on a day when he does not expect him, at a time he does not know. He will punish him severely and rank him among the undeserving to trust.

Luke 13:03 But I tell you, you will all come to the same end unless you reform.

Luke 13:24–27 Many I tell you will try to enter and be unable. When once the master of the house has risen to lock the door and you stand outside knocking and saying, "Sir, open for us", "I do not know where you come from." Then you will begin to say,"We ate and drank in your company. You taught in our streets" But he answered," I tell you, I do not know where you come from. Away from me, you evildoers!"

Luke 13:30 Some who are last will be first and some who are first will be last.

Luke 14:26 If anyone comes to me without turning his back on his father and mother, his wife and his children, his brothers and sisters, indeed his very self, he cannot be my follower.

Luke 14:27 Anyone who does not take up his cross and follow me cannot be my disciple.

Luke 14:33 In the same way, none of you can be my disciple if he does not renounce all his possessions.

Luke 14:34-35 Salt is good, but if salt looses it's flavor what good is it for seasoning? It is fit for neither the soil nor the manure heap; it has to be thrown away.

Luke 16:13 You cannot give yourself to God and money.

John 3:18 Whoever does not believe is already condemned.

John 12:48 Whoever rejects me and does not accept my words already has his judge, namely the word I have spoken - it is that which will condemn him on the last day.

John 13:8 Peter replied, You shall never wash my feet! If I do not wash you, Jesus answered, you will not share in my heritage.

John 15:6 A man who does not live in me is like a withered, rejected branch, picked up to be thrown in the fire and burnt.

Romans 2:5–8 God will be revealed, wrath and fury to those who selfishly disobey the truth and obey wickedness.

Romans 2:9 Yes, affliction and anguish will come upon every man who has done evil

Romans 8:13 If you live according to the flesh, you will die

1 Corinthians 2:6 Is it not a wisdom of this age, however, not of the rulers of this age, who are men headed for destruction.

1 Corinthians 3:16–17 Are you not aware that you are the temple of God, and that the Spirit of God dwells in you? If anyone destroys God's temple, God will destroy him.

2 Corinthians 5:10 The lives of all of us are to be revealed before the tribunal of Christ so that each one may receive his recompense, good or bad, according to his life in the body.

Galatians 5:19–21 It is obvious what proceeds from the flesh: lewd conduct, impurity, licentiousness, idolatry, sorcery, hostility, bickering, jealousy, outbursts of rage, selfish rivalries, dissentions, factions, envy, drunkenness, orgies, and the like. I warn you, as I have warned you before: those who do such things will not inherit the kingdom of God!

Galatians 6:7 A man will reap only what he sows.

Ephesians 5:5 Make no mistake about this: no fornicator, no unclean or lustful person—in effect an idolater—has any inheritance in the kingdom of Christ and of God.

2 Thessalonians 1:8–9 with flaming power he will inflict punishment on those who do not acknowledge God nor heed the good news of our Lord Jesus. Such as these will suffer the penalty of eternal ruin apart from the presence of the Lord and the Glory of his might

2 Thessalonians 2:11–12 Therefore God is sending among them a perverse spirit which will lead them to give credence to falsehood, so that all who have not believed the truth but have delighted in evildoing will be condemned.

1 Timothy 3:6 He should not be a new convert, lest he become conceited and thus incur the punishment once meted out to the devil.

1 Timothy 5:24 Some men's sins are fragrant and cry out for judgment.

2 Timothy 2:12 But if we deny him, he will deny us.

Hebrew 2:2 and all transgression and disobedience receive its due punishment

Hebrew 4:6 Therefore, since it remains for some to enter, and those to whom it was first announced did not because of unbelief

Hebrew 10:27 only a fearful expectation of judgement and a flaming fire to consume the adversaries of God.

Hebrew 10:29–30 Do you not suppose that a much worse punishment is due to man who disdains the Son of God, thinks the covenant-blood by which he was sanctified to be ordinary, and insults the Spirit of grace? We know who said Vengeance is mine; I will repay

Hebrew 12:25 how much greater punishment will be ours if we turn away from him who speaks from heaven!

James 2:13 Merciless is the judgement on a man who has not shown mercy

2 Peter 2:12 Because of their decadence they too will be destroyed, suffering the reward of their wickedness.

1 John 3:8 The man who sins belongs to the devil

1 John 3:15 you know that eternal life abides in no murder's heart.

Jude1:4 godless types, long ago destined for the condemnation I shall describe

Revelation 2:23 I will give each of you what your conduct deserves.

Revelation 20:15 anyone whose name was not found inscribe in the book of the living was hurled into the fire.

Revelation 21:8 As the cowards and the traitors to the faith, depraved and the murderers, the fornicators and sorcerers, the idol-worshipers and deceivers of every sort—their lot is a fiery pool of burning sulfur, the second death!

Revelation 22:12 Remember, I am coming soon! I bring with me the reward that will be given to each man as is conduct deserves.

How do the condemned get to hell?

Matthew 5:13 Then it is good for nothing but to be thrown out and trampled underfoot.

Matthew 12:36 I assure you, on judgement day people will be held accountable for every unguarded word they speak.

Matthew 12:37 and by your words you will be condemned.

Matthew 13:30 First collect the weeds and bundle them up to burn

Matthew 13:40 Just as weeds are collected and burned, so will it be at the end of the world.

Matthew 13:42 The angel will hurl them into a fiery furnace where they will wail and grind their teeth.

Matthew 13:49–50 That is how it will be at the end of the world. Angels will go out and separate the wicked from the just and hurl the wicked into the fiery furnace, where they will wail and grind their teeth.

Matthew 16:27 The Son of Man will come with his Father's glory accompanied by his angels. When he does, he will repay each man according to his conduct.

Matthew 21:43 For this reason, I tell you, the kingdom of God will be taken away from you and given to a nation that will yield a rich harvest.

Matthew 22:07 At this the king grew furious and sent his army to destroy those murderers and burn their cities

Matthew 22:13–14 Bind him hand and foot and throw him out into the night to wail and grind his teeth. The invited are many, the elected are few.

Matthew 25:10–12 Then the door was barred. Later the other bridesmaid came back. Master Master! they cried. Open the door for us. But he answered, I tell you, I do not know you.

Matthew 25:30 Throw this worthless servant into the darkness outside, where he can wail and grind his teeth.

Matthew 25:41 Then he will say to those on his left: "Out of my sight, you condemned, into the everlasting fire prepared for the devil and his angels."

Matthew 25:46 These will go off into eternal punishment

Luke 3:9 Every tree that is not fruitful will be cut down and thrown into the fire.

Luke 12:40 Be on your guard therefore. The son of man will come when you least expect him.

Luke 19:27 Now about those enemies of mine who do not want me to be king, bring them in and slay them in my presence.

John 5:28–29 for the hour is coming in which all those in their tombs shall hear his voice and come forth the evildoers shall rise to be damned.

Jude 1:14–15 See, the Lord has come with his countless holy ones about him to pass judgement on all men, indicating the Godless for every evil deed they have done, and convicting those Godless sinners of every harsh word they have uttered against him.

Revelation 3:7 The Holy One, the True, who wields David's key…who closes and no one can open

Revelation 20:3 The angel hurled him into the abyss

Revelation 20:14 Then the death and the nether world were hurled into the pool of fire, which is the second death;

What is it like in hell?

Matthew 3:12 but the chaff he will burn in unquenchable fire.

Mathew 5:29 Better to lose part of your body than to have it all cast into Gehenna.

Mathew 8:12 Wailing will be heard there, and the grinding of teeth.

Mathew 13:12 the man who has not, will lose what little he has.

Matthew 18:8–9 Better to enter life maimed or crippled than to be thrown with two hands or two feet into endless fire. Better to enter life with one eye than to be thrown with both into fiery Gehenna.

Marc 9:43 enter Gehena with its unquenchable fire.

Marc 9:48 where the worms die not and the fire is never extinguished

Luke 10:14 It will go easier on the day of judgement for Tyre and Sidon than for you.

Luke 13:28 There will be wailing and grinding of teeth when you see Abraham, Isaac, Jacob, and all the prophets safe in the kingdom of God, and you yourself rejected.

Luke 14:24 But I tell you that not one of those invited shall taste a morsel of my dinner.

Luke 16:23–25 From the abode of the dead where he was in torment, he raised his eyes and saw Abraham afar off, and Lazarus resting in his bosom. He called out , "Father Abraham, have pity, have pity on me. Send Lazarus to dip his finger in water to refresh my tongue, for I am tortured in these flames. My child, ' replied Abraham, 'remember that you were well off in your lifetime, while Lazarus was in misery. Now he has found consolation here, but you have found torment.

Luke 16:26 Between you and us there is fixed a great abyss, so that those who might wish to cross from here to you cannot do so, nor can anyone cross from your side to us.

Luke 16:27–28 Father, I ask you, then, the rich man said, send him to my fathers house where I have five brothers. Let him be a warning to them so that they may not end in this place of torment.

Luke 17:1–2 Scandals will inevitably arise, but woe to him through whom they come. He would be better off thrown into the sea with a millstone around his neck than giving scandal to one of these little ones.

Jude 1:7 They are set before us, as they undergo a punishment of eternal fire.

Revelation 9:1-2 The star was given the key to the shaft of the abyss; he opened it and smoke poured out of the shaft like the smoke from an enormous furnace.

Revelation 14:10-11 He will be tormented in burning sulfur before the holy angels and before the lamb, and the smoke of their torment shall rise forever. There shall be no relief day or night for those who worship the beast or it's image or accept the mark of its name.

Revelation 19:20 Both were hurled down alive into the fiery pool of burning sulfur.

Revelation 20:10 The devil who led them astray was hurled into the pool of burning sulfur, where the beast and the false prophet had also been thrown. There they will be tortured day and night, forever and ever.

Chapter 4

Recommendations on How to Get to Heaven

Recommendations

God loves us so much that he came on earth as a man to provide us with a manual, in a manner of speaking, to teach us how to get to Heaven. He showed us a way to live our lives that will lead not only to fulfillment in this life, but to everlasting joy in the next. He also provides divine help or strength in the form of graces to enable us to follow his ways and avoid evil temptations.

The Ten Commandments

1 – I, the lord, am your God…You shall not have other gods besides me.

2 – You shall not take the name of the Lord, your God in vain.

3 – Remember to keep holy the Sabbath day.

4 – Honor your Father and Mother.

5 – You shall not kill.

6 – You shall not commit adultery.

7 – You shall not steal.

8 – You shall not bear false witness against your neighbor.

9 – You shall not covet your neighbor's wife.

10 – You shall not covet your neighbor's house.

Adapted from Exodus 20:2
and placed in this order by St. Augustine

Precepts of the Church

Jesus spoke to Simon (Peter) as follows:

Matthew 16:18 I for my part declare to you, you are 'Rock,' and on this rock I will build my church, and the jaws of death shall not prevail against it. I will entrust to you the keys of the kingdom of heaven. Whatever you declare bound on earth shall be bound in heaven; whatever you declare loosed on earth shall be loosed in heaven.

1 – Assist at Mass on Sundays and Holy Days of obligation.

2 – Fast and abstain on the days appointed.

3 – Confess your sins at least once a year.

4 – Receive Holy Communion during Easter time.

5 – Contribute to the support of the Church.

6 – Observe the laws of the Church concerning marriage.

Sacraments

The Lord, because he loves and cares so much for us, has left us with the tremendous assistance we need in the form of graces. Graces are gifts from God—most powerful gifts. The sacraments are a direct method of obtaining these graces.

Sacraments are actions of Christ on our soul. They are channels or streams flowing from the open side of Christ through Mary's hands to us. There are 7 sacraments and each provides a special grace with a particular purpose.

Baptism: birth in the life of grace.

Confirmation: gives us power to become adults in the life of grace.

Penance: is the medicine of the soul to heal sin.

Holy Eucharist: the Flesh and Blood of Christ as the food and drink of our soul.

Matrimony: a man and woman bind themselves for life and receive the grace to discharge their duties.

Holy Orders: provides priests to teach and sanctify the Mystical Body.

Extreme Unction (Anointing of the Sick): fully restores the health of a soul lost by sin.

Virtues

What a treasure we have in the Rosary. St. Louis De Montfort said, 'The more we honor the Blessed Virgin, the more we honor Jesus Christ.' The 'MISSION' of the Rosary is to help us realize the purpose of our existence and the importance of applying the 'lessons' of the Gospel in our daily lives.

The Church, over the centuries, has attached a series of virtues to each of the 15 decades of the Rosary. These virtues are so very pleasing to God that, by the growth that comes with their practice, we receive the gifts of ever-increasing inner peace and spiritual fortitude. The Lord has left us goals. The following are based on centuries of meditations and tradition.

Joyful Mysteries
Annunciation *Humility*
Visitation *Charity*
Nativity *Poverty*
Presentation *Obedience*
Finding Jesus *Appreciation*

Sorrowful Mysteries
    Agony *Contrition*
    Scourging *Purity*
    Crown of Thorns *Courage*
    Carrying of the Cross *Patience*
    Crucifixion *Love*

Glorious Mysteries
    Resurrection *Faith*
    Ascension *Hope*
    Holy Spirit *Enthusiasm*
    Assumption *Holy Death*
    Crowning of Mary *Our Queen*

Chapter 5

Spiritual Thoughts

Love

1 Corinthians 13:4
Love is patient and kind; love is not jealous, or conceited, or proud; love is not ill-mannered, or selfish, or irritable; love does not keep a record of wrongs; love is not happy with evil, but is happy with the truth. Love never gives up: its faith, hope, and patience never fail.

Reflection
In our lives, Jesus calls us to love: to love ourselves, to love others and to let ourselves be loved. The challenge comes in difficult situations. Two examples come to mind: when we are wronged; when we or our values are threatened.

When faced with these situations, loving the offending person does not mean that we sweep the problem under the carpet and pretend that it does not exist. Nor do we give in and let the other person have his way. Avoiding these issues only leads to further ills. On the contrary, love calls us to deal with these situations with immense charity and kindness, and at the same time, with assertiveness and determination. To respond to this call, we need strength of courage and of will.

If limited to human strength, the appropriate response is an impossible task, yes. But, with God's help, with his guiding hand and with his supernatural grace, we are enabled to love.

What we choose to believe when we choose to be Catholic

The Apostles' Creed prayer has been in existence for 2000 years. I stand in awe of the fact that this prayer has been unchanged and repeated for 20 centuries. Tradition ascribes this Creed to the Apostles themselves. It was put into written words around the end of the 1st century. It was, and still is, the prayer said at Baptism.

Apostles' Creed

> I believe in God,
> the Father almighty,
> Creator of heaven and earth,
> and in Jesus Christ, his only Son, our Lord,
> who was conceived by the Holy Spirit,
> born of the Virgin Mary,
> suffered under Pontius Pilate,
> was crucified, died and was buried;
> he descended into hell;
> on the third day he rose again from the dead;

he ascended into heaven,
and is seated at the right hand of God the Father almighty;
from there he will come to judge the living and the dead.
I believe in the Holy Spirit,
the Holy Catholic Church,
the communion of saints,
the forgiveness of sins,
the resurrection of the body,
and life everlasting. Amen.

The modern version of the Nicene Creed has its origins in the Council of Nicene in the year 325AD. It was finalized at the Council of Constantinople in 381AD. The Creed was needed to counteract the Arius heresy being spread at the time that Jesus Christ was not really God.

Nicene Creed

We believe in one God,
the Father, the Almighty,
maker of heaven and earth,
of all that is, seen and unseen.
We believe in one Lord, Jesus Christ,
the only Son of God,
eternally begotten of the Father,
God from God, Light from Light,
true God from true God,
begotten, not made,

of one Being with the Father.
Through Him all things were made.
For us and for our salvation
He came down from heaven:
by the power of the Holy Spirit
He became incarnate from the Virgin Mary,
and was made man.
For our sake He was crucified under Pontius Pilate;
He suffered death and was buried.
On the third day He rose again
in accordance with the Scriptures;
He ascended into heaven
and is seated at the right hand of the Father.
He will come again in glory to judge the living and the dead,
and His kingdom will have no end.
We believe in the Holy Spirit, the Lord, the giver of life,
who proceeds from the Father.*
With the Father and the Son He is worshiped and glorified.
He has spoken through the Prophets.
We believe in one holy catholic and apostolic Church.
We acknowledge one baptism for the forgiveness of sins.
We look for the resurrection of the dead,
and the life of the world to come. AMEN.

The Eucharist

When the priest pronounces Jesus's divine words at the Consecration during the Holy Mass, "This is my body…This is the chalice of my Blood" (Matt. 26: 26-27), the bread and wine become the Body and Blood of Jesus. The bread and wine no longer exist, having been transubstantiated (transformed) into the divine Body and Blood. "My Flesh is real food and my Blood is real drink" (John 6:56).

Jesus gave each person born a gift that is incomprehensible in its charity because: he holds us special and precious; he considers us deserving; he loves us so much. Having knowledge of the struggles and difficulties we would face during our earthly journey and having knowledge of the super human powers that the Evil One (Satan) has over us, Jesus made himself available to each of us. Those of us that accept his gift of the Eucharist into our bodies become part of Him and receive His assistance, His power, His fortitude and His wisdom. These become part of our soul, part of our flesh and blood, part of us.

What did this gift cost Jesus?

God, the Creator of all things took flesh from our Holy Mother Mary, with her consent, and came to live among us. Why? He cares for us so much that he chose to come in person to teach us, and provide guidance and help. Further, he chose to make himself available throughout time in the Eucharist.

But he even went a step further. He suffered a cruel and agonizing death on our behalf. He offered his torturous suffering and death for us so we would have the assistance and guidance we need at our disposal. The greatest benefit we receive from Jesus's cruel suffering is his availability to every individual by way of the Eucharist.

What is our responsibility?

Through authority given by God and through the guidance of the Holy Spirit, the Church has taught us how to approach and receive the Eucharist in a manner pleasing to Almighty God. Each person is required to receive with the utmost respect, and in a profoundly responsible manner. Our Church has provided Divinely inspired guidelines on how this is to be done. To be disobedient to the following guidelines is a grievous sin, a most serious breech of respect and an act of defiance against Almighty God.

Since the Eucharist is the Body of Christ Himself Who is true God and true Man, we are bound by the First Commandment to revere and adore Him. Each and every fragment of the Host is the 'true Body of Christ.' We have to take every precaution to insure that no fragment of the Host is dropped when we receive Holy Communion.

One of the seven official conditions written by the Sacred Congregation for Divine Worship reads: 'Whatever manner is adopted, one must take care to not drop or lose any particles of the Eucharistic Bread, one must take care to see that the hands are suitably clean, and that there be observed the proper composure of gestures according to the customs of the various peoples.'

The Eucharist is for Catholics only. If non-Catholics wish to receive, they must convert to the Catholic faith first.

A person must be in the state of grace to receive the Eucharist. Therefore, someone who has committed a serious sin must make a confession (reconciliation) to a priest to obtain forgiveness before receiving the Eucharist. To receive voluntarily in the state of serious sin, with full knowledge and intent, is itself a very serious sin (an act of defiance) against the Church and against God. God always gives us a chance, always gives us a way out, always wants to forgive—no matter how serious the sin. All we have to do is take advantage of his generosity and be truly sorry for our sins.

Catholics who have not made a minimum commitment to weekly Saturday evening or Sunday Mass are instructed to refrain from receiving Holy Communion. Couples living together outside of the sacrament of Marriage are instructed to seek spiritual direction before receiving Holy Communion.

The Stations of the Cross

The Stations of the Cross is a ritual acknowledgment of events leading to Christ's crucifixion and resurrection. These fourteen events can be found depicted on plaques in Catholic Churches and Holy places of worship throughout the world. Insight and growth is gained by examining the attitudes and values represented at each event and attempting to understand and implement these in our lives. Meditating on the Stations of the Cross to gain Christian insight and to grow in our Christian way of life has been part of the Catholic tradition for many centuries.

The fourteen Stations are:

1) Jesus bears his cross

2) Jesus falls for the first time

3) Jesus meets his mother

4) Simon helps Jesus

5) Veronica wipes the face of Jesus

6) Jesus falls the second time

7) Jesus speaks to the women

8) Jesus falls the third time

9) Jesus is stripped of his garment

10) Jesus is nailed to the cross

11) Jesus dies on the cross

12) Jesus is taken down from the cross

13) Jesus is laid in the tomb

14) Jesus rises from the dead

Forgiveness

Dictionary Definition
to grant pardon for or remission of; to cease to blame or feel resentment against; to remit, as a debt; to show forgiveness; to grant pardon.

Reflection
At times we have all asked ourselves, 'if only I had a second chance.' The Lord Jesus, our God, thinks we are so special, so worthwhile, that he always gives us a second, a third, a fourth…an infinite number of chances. He sets no limit on the number of times he is willing to forgive us, no matter what we have done. No sin is so bad that our Lord Jesus, our God, will not grant us forgiveness. He is always ready, happy and willing to grant us forgiveness. If only we understood the tremendous gift that was passed on to us through the Sacrament of reconciliation.

Matthew 18:12–13 "Tell me. Suppose a man has a hundred sheep and one of them strays; will he not leave the ninety-nine on the hillside and go search for the stray? I tell you solemnly, if he finds it, it gives him more joy than do the ninety-nine that did not stray at all"

Luke 11:14 If you, with all your sins, know how to give your children good things, how much more will the heavenly Father give the Holy Spirit to those who ask him.

Luke 11:36 Be compassionate, as your Father is compassionate.

Luke 23:34 Father, forgive them; they do not know what they are doing.

1 John 1:9 But if we acknowledge our sins, he who is just can be trusted to forgive our sins.

Mark 2:5 When Jesus saw their faith, he said to the paralyzed man, "My son, your sins are forgiven."

Luke 7:48 He said to her then, "Your sins are forgiven", at which his fellow guest began to ask among themselves, "Who is this that he even forgives sins?" Meanwhile he said to the women, "Your faith has been your salvation. Now go in peace."

Mark 3:28:29 I give you my word, every sin will be forgiven mankind and all the blasphemes men utter, but whoever blasphemes against the Holy Spirit will never be forgiven.

Mark 4:12 so they will look intently and not see, listen carefully and not understand. lest perhaps they repent and be forgiven."

Luke 6:37 Pardon, and you shall be pardon.

Luke 8:47 I tell you, that is why her many sins are forgiven - because of her great love. Little is forgiven the one whose love is small.

Acts 8:22 Reform you evil ways. Pray that the Lord pardon you for thinking the way you have.

Colossians 3:13 Even when you were dead in sin and your flesh was uncircumcised, God gave you new life in company with Christ. He pardoned all your sins.

James 5:15 If he has committed any sins, forgiveness will be his. Hence declare your sins to one another, and pray for one another that you may find healing.

1 John 2:12 Little ones, I address you, for through his Name your sins have been forgiven.

Acts 5:31 He whom God has exalted at his right hand as ruler and savior is to bring repentance to Israel and forgiveness of sins.

Acts 13:38 you must realize, my brothers, that it is through him that the forgiveness of sins is being proclaimed to you, including the remission of all those charges you could never be acquitted of under the law of Moses.

Acts 26:18 to open the eyes of those to whom I am sending you, to turn them from darkness to light and from the dominion of Satan to God; that through their faith in me they may obtain the forgiveness of their sins and a portion among God's people.

Ephesians 1:7 It is in Christ and through his blood that we have been redeemed and our sins forgiven

Colossians 1:14 Through him we have redemption, the forgiveness of our sins.

Luke 11:4 Forgive us our sins for we too forgive all who do us wrong;

Scapular

Wearing a Scapular is an assurance of salvation. "Whosoever dies clothed in this [Scapular] shall not suffer eternal fire." This is Mary's Promise made July 16, 1251 to Saint Simon Stock.

A Scapular, then, has a deep meaning. It is a rich present brought down from Heaven by Our Lady

Herself. "Wear it devoutly and perseveringly," She says to each soul. "It is My garment. To be clothed in it means you are continually thinking of Me, and I in turn, am always thinking of you and helping you secure eternal life."

St. Alphonsus says, "Just as men take pride in having others wear their livery, so the Most Holy Mary is pleased when Her servants wear Her Scapular as a mark that they have dedicated themselves to Her service, and are members of the Family of the Mother of God."

Pope Benedict XV granted an indulgence of 500 days each time the Scapular is kissed. So, if you don't already have one, go and get one and wear it faithfully.

Steps to Serenity and Peace with God and Ourselves

1) Admit we are powerless to overcome our sinfulness and difficulties by ourselves

2) Believe that the intercession of our Blessed Lady and the Communion of Saints can restore us to ever-increasing inner strength and serenity

3) Decide to turn our will and our lives over to the care of our Lord Jesus Christ and our Blessed Mother Mary

4) Frequently take fearless moral inventory of ourselves by examining our conscience with honesty and responsibility

5) Admit to God, to ourselves and to a priest in the sacrament of Reconciliation (Confession) the exact nature of our wrongs

6) Be prepared to take the steps necessary to earn forgiveness for our wrongdoing, regardless of the severity

7) Humbly ask God through the intercession of our Blessed Mother and the communion of Saints to remove our shortcomings

8) List all the people we have harmed and be willing to make amends to them all

9) Make direct amends to such people whenever possible, except when it would injure them or others

10) Continue to take personal inventory and when we have done wrong, promptly admit it.

11) Continue using the sacrament of reconciliation (confession) to take advantage of the special and effective graces and assistance God has provided through this sacrament

12) Attempt to find a sponsor, a special person in whom you can confide

13) Tell your life's story to a special person who you believe can give you encouragement and guidance

14) Seek, through prayer and meditation, to improve our conscious contact with God, praying only for the knowledge of his will for us and the power to carry it out

Teaching on Contraception

Catechism of the Catholic Church

"Periodic continence, that is, the methods of birth regulation based on self-observation and the use of infertile periods, is in conformity with the objective criteria of morality.
   In contrast, every action which, whether in anticipation of the conjugal act, or an end or as a means, to render procreation impossible is intrinsically evil."

The sexual act must take place exclusively within marriage. Outside of marriage it always constitutes a grave sin and excludes one from sacramental communion.

Humanae Vitae

"Equally to be condemned, as the magisterium of the Church has affirmed on many occasions, is direct sterilization, whether of man or of the women, whether permanent or temporary"

In other words; artificial contraception is intrinsically evil and therefore a sin. In contrast, using natural family method for legitimate reasons is acceptable to regulate birth.

Encyclical of Pope Paul VI on the Regulation of Birth – July 25, 1968

Conforming to the teachings

The following website presents a method of natural contraception that can be in conformity with the teachings of the Catholic Church.
http://www.billings-centre.ab.ca/

One Master

Mathew 6:24 No man can serve two masters. He will hate one and love the other or be attentive to one and despise the other. You cannot give yourself to God and money.

Interpretation

This world presents to us a mixture of good and evil values. Our prayer and hope is for the Holy Spirit of God to provide us with the wisdom to know the difference and the strength to choose good over evil.

An Interesting Article

According to recent polls, large numbers of Catholics disagree with the teaching of their church on contraception, premarital sex and matters of sexual morality. Let's put this in perspective. If these polls had been available on the eve of Christ's life, he most certainly would have been advised to change His message or risk being seen as out of touch with reality. Christ was not concerned with popularity and his teaching were not popular. They were not popular then and they are not popular now

Conclusion

I remember how religion was taught when I was in grade school. We were provided a Catechism that was divided into a number of important religious topics. They presented clear answers to important questions. Gaining knowledge on these topics is as important today as it was then. Today the question-and-answer teaching method has been completely eliminated. This change has resulted in the younger generation having a serious lack of knowledge with regards to important aspects of Catholic teaching. One of a number of examples is that many young Catholics are not aware of Purgatory and how prayers help those souls that are in Purgatory. I felt the need to write clear and concise information on Catholic topics that do not seem to be insufficiently propagated.

Basic knowledge about the teachings of the Catholic Church is essential to its members. I hope that this book will provide the reader with necessary information and a clearer understanding of many aspects of Catholic teachings.

We need to remember that Jesus Christ is the Founder of the Catholic Church and promised to remain with his Church until the end of time.